What people are saying about

JAMIE GEORGE...

"I look forward to my conversation with Jamie every week. I couldn't ask for more from my coach, with thoughtful and timely advice he enhances my ability to execute and brings out the best in me!"

Kyle Wailes
CEO, Wellvana

"Jamie has come alongside me giving direction insight and life guidance when I was critically in need. His empathy and positivity have inspired me to walk boldly ahead with confidence and clarity!"

Joel Smallbone
Grammy Award Winning Band
For King & Country

"Jamie has coached me through challenges in friendships, business relationships, in marriage and parenting. While conflict cannot be avoided, it can be managed. The tools in this book will transform the way you interact with everyone."

Dustin Hillis

CEO Southwestern Family of Companies

"Jamie has been instrumental in helping me navigate through all of my life changes. He has helped me start a business, deepen my relationship with my children, and helped me understand my husband better. I have grown spiritually and emotionally over the last year with Jamie's help. He is a truly gifted coach and mentor."

Yvonne Patton

Nurse & Business Owner

"Jamie leads with profound questions and has always reminded me that, no matter how messy it gets, it all belongs. I better understand my value, I'm more whole, more free and just overall more alive since my coaching with Mr. George."

Tyler Ward

Artist & Founder of *The Song House*

"Jamie and I live on opposite sides of the earth, yet our stories have connected. Australians value truth and compassion. We don't care what you know until we know that you care. Jamie's writing has truth and grace, a prophetic edge and a shepherd's heart."

Graham Mabury

Radio Personality

The Thrivalist Handbook, How to Stop
Surviving and Start Thriving in Your
Relationships, Work, and Life

Published by Story Collector Inc.
Nashville, Tennessee USA

9798356447457 ISBN
© 2022 Jamie George

Printed in the United States of America First
Edition 2022 ISBN: 9798356447457

DEDICATION

*To my Mastermind collaborators,
thank you for reminding me we are all being
formed from the same clay.*

TABLE OF CONTENTS

INTRODUCTION

Expectations are the stories we believe about how others will behave. And how often we are confronted with unmet expectations!

We try to figure out ways to get other people to change. We spend tremendous amounts of time and energy trying to fix and adjust other people's behavior. Frustrated and emotionally spent, we find ourselves unsuccessful and unhappy.

Have you been there?

Are you there right now?

- Do you feel overwhelmed?

- Do you feel like giving up?

- Do relationships seem complex and overwhelming to you?

- Do you feel exhausted trying to keep up with other people's expectations?

Here is the good news! Every difficulty
you have is a cover-up of one
foundational problem: resentment.

All expectations are premeditated
resentments.

You are the victim of your own unmet
expectations. Every day that you live as
a victim, you suffer—and your
relationships suffer.

Let the suffering cease. Let the repair begin. It is time for healing, wholeness, and restoration.

It is time to identify those patterns and begin thriving in relationships in ways you never imagined. Let us stop the toxic habits of relating, and instead learn how to become a Thrivalist!

You are going to release resentment. Old relationships will be transformed, and new relationships will germinate.

You will discover that love holds no record of wrong.

The resentment you feel for your own failures and the failures of others is keeping you stuck. This book is inviting you to bring an end to your suffering.

Suffering is a choice.

Pain is something that we cannot avoid, but how we view pain and how we view failure has everything to do with whether we spend our days experiencing heaven or experiencing hell.

We are all conditioned.

We have all received programming—
from our family of origin, from our birth
order, from our religious or non-
religious upbringing, and from our
culture. This does not make us wrong; it
is how our childlike wildness was
domesticated so we could function
socially within a given set of parameters.

As human beings, we have free will, agency, choice.

We have the capacity to shift, adjust, and choose a different mindset. We get to evolve and change our way of being in the world.

New information, especially *inspiring* new information, often encourages us and motivates us toward transformation. However, it is hard to teach an old dog new tricks. You can lead a horse to water, but you can't make it *think*.

We are resistant to change and we often prefer comfort to uncertainty.

Until finally there is that magical moment when we become tired of suffering. The wounds are just too much, and it is finally time to stop the bleeding.

Perhaps that is why this book has found its way to you.

You want more.

You are done playing small.

You are worn out from carrying everyone else.

You are tired of the shame, fear, hurt, and anger—or you are just plain tired.

This book is meant to be a reprieve for your soul, a salve for your heart, and a jolt to your mind.

The first step is recognizing that something needs to change.

You can't heal what you don't acknowledge, and you can't acknowledge what you can't see.

Sometimes a word, a phrase, or a story gives sight to the blind. Many people are held captive in unlocked cages. The only thing they need in order to gain freedom is to have someone point out to them that the door is unlocked. That's my job.

The answers are already in you.

This book is just meant to shine a spotlight on where you are stuck and where you want to be free. It is meant to give words to your experience and motion to your dreams.

HOW TO USE THIS BOOK

Grab a red marker and green marker and outline the appropriate triangles as you go. And grab a pen. This book is designed for you to interact with it. Plenty of space has been left for you to journal comments, thoughts, and feelings. Let this book be a companion for you as you take simple steps into deeper love and connection with those relationships that matter most.

With clarity comes empowerment, and with empowerment comes responsibility; and in the words of Peter Parker's Uncle Ben (or Voltaire, who supposedly said it first), "With great power comes great responsibility."

Let's begin your Thrivalist journey by identifying some simple words that reflect how we relate to one another, especially in conflict.

THE
RED TRIANGLE

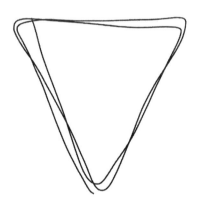

In 1968, psychologist Dr. Stephen Karpman developed a social model known as the Drama Triangle. It deals with how we relate to others in unhealthy ways. Each point on the triangle has a label. These labels have varied throughout the years, but the ones most consistent with my observations on human behavior are these:

RESCUER   PERPETRATOR

VICTIM

Since the ego seeks survival at all costs, the Drama Triangle reflects our most primitive way of interacting.

Most of us will find that we spend the majority of our time on one corner of the triangle. It is our dominant strategy for emotional safety.

True to its name, the Drama Triangle is all drama all the time. Another name for this triangle is the Red Triangle, as it is a home for the flushed face of anger and resentment.

It is also an enclosed shape where emotional violence, and sometimes even physical violence fills the space.

In this "Red" way of being, we connect with others through intensity rather than through intimacy.

We evade being vulnerable, and we avoid revealing our true selves (more about our true selves later). Instead, we stay in a protective posture, quick to move from one point of the triangle to another when the situation demands.

Each position on the Red Triangle has one goal: to avoid taking responsibility.

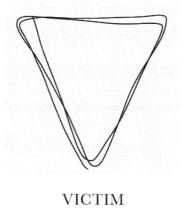

VICTIM

At the bottom of the triangle is the Victim. The victim might be someone who has fashioned a story about how someone else hurt them, or the victim might be someone who legitimately experienced abuse or tragedy.

Examples of this would be someone who has or had a disease, someone who was abused as a child, someone who has experienced great loss, or someone who was unjustly accused. The pain and trauma of that experience matters.

Therapists remind us that the moment we were perpetrated by a person or a circumstance we were a victim. The next moment, we were not. This is tremendously empowering.

When someone gets stuck, shaping his identity around his victimization he loses his power and autonomy.

Blaming, whining, complaining, and deflecting are common ways of being. He uses catastrophic language that is consistently part of the narrative.

Phrases such as

always,

nothing,

never, and

every time

are frequently used to prevent others
from challenging or countering the
victim's story about why he can't
change.

This warm blanket of self-pity works for a time. There are others who find him and sympathize with his pain and who validate it, merge with it, or try to fix it. This feels good. He is not required to do anything except refine his victim story so that it seems even more dramatic the next time he tells it.

The pheromones, or "chemical vibrations," created and released by the victim are an alluring invitation for the closest rescuer. The victim is always looking for someone to rescue him, and he is often unknowingly cutting a psychological deal with the rescuer.

(Use your smartphone camera to scan this QR Code to listen in on an interview with one of my clients discussing victimization!)

RESCUER

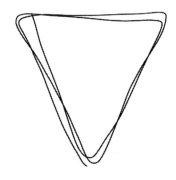

The Rescuer wants to be noble, enjoys the role of hero, and wants to find self-worth in self-sacrifice, martyrdom, and the drama of "saving the day." The rescuer often dislikes tension, so he rushes in to make peace to resolve the discomfort. While these traits might be healthy and appropriate in certain contexts, on the Drama Triangle, they are harmful to the relationship.

Psychologists use the term "codependent" to describe the person who finds his well-being lassoed to the well-being of someone else.

"If you're not okay, I'm not okay."

That is the classic mantra of someone who is codependent. Spiritual teachers use the term "attachment" to describe the same kind of energy.

Anthony de Mello writes, "The tragedy of an attachment is that if its object is not attained it causes unhappiness. But if it is attained, it does not cause happiness—it merely causes a flash of pleasure followed by weariness, and it is always accompanied, of course, by the anxiety that you may lose the object of your attachment."[1]

The rescuer's need to be needed finds him overfunctioning to save the victim from unwanted stress, discomfort, struggle, and inconvenience.

The problem is that most of us experience our greatest growth in the midst of struggle and challenge. The rescuer becomes the obstacle for growth in the victim.

The victim feeds the rescuer's desire to feel heroic, and the rescuer feeds the victim's desire to avoid taking responsibility.

Every complaint is a vision—a vision of possibility—of what could be.

Instead of the victim having space to ask himself, "What in me wants to emerge?" the rescuer validates the victim's complaint and chooses to carry the burden for the victim.

While there are times it is appropriate to support someone and meet their needs, doing so from a craving to be seen or a desire to remove tension stunts the growth of the rescuer and hamstrings the victim, delaying the capability of each of them to stand on their own two feet.

Speaking at a conference a few years ago, I was involved in an exercise with couples. Everyone in the room was asked to stand and hug their partner.

They were to hold their hug for thirty seconds.

They were then to end the hug, face the front of the room, and reflect on their embrace. In particular, they were to consider their posture while they were hugging.

After some thought, one woman said that her husband had leaned all his weight on her, causing her to prop herself up against a chair in order to hold herself up. One man said that he felt his wife pulling him toward her with such force that he could barely keep his balance.

In both cases, no one was standing securely on their own two feet.

This exercise is a great image to show how few of us know how to stand securely on our own. The temptation is to turn to dependence (you are responsible for me), codependence (if you're not okay, I'm not okay), or independence (I can live life on my own).

Whether in a romantic relationship, a parenting relationship, or a friendship, the aim is *inter*dependence. When you are in an interdependent relationship you honor the autonomy in the other. You confidently show up both for yourself and for the other person without losing yourself in the relationship.

Esther Perel says that the truest form of love is experienced in "the ability to stay connected to one's self in the presence of another."[2]

The rescuer has trouble with this since his identity is enmeshed in the life of the other person.

After all, who would he be without someone to rescue?

(Scan this QR Code to listen in on an interview with one of my clients discussing being a rescuer!)

PERPETRATOR

Many of us find relationships that
complement our preferred drama style
of relating. We cut a (usually
subconscious) psychological deal with
the other person as a way of connecting.

The victim wants to avoid taking action,
and the rescuer wants to feel needed and
important. Eventually however, the
victim and the rescuer get worn out from
the dance.

The rescuer gets frustrated by the behavior of the victim and the victim gets angry with the behavior of the rescuer. The energy shifts and she starts becoming controlling and vindictive, demeaning the other person with words and actions. She changes positions on the triangle and becomes the Perpetrator.

The ego is fully on display as it engages fight mode, stonewalling indifference, or sneaky payback.

In the perpetrator position, what is communicated as justice is simply a cloaking device to deploy revenge. Violent outbursts, as well as silence and abrupt exits, are common ways to make the other person pay.

Rather than take responsibility for her behavior, the perpetrator keeps the other person at arm's length. It is very important to the perpetrator that the other person is punished for what he has done.

Feeling justified and in the seat of superiority, she berates and belittles him, judging him for his wrongdoing. The perpetrator believes she is right and that everyone else is wrong, and she uses violence with her words and actions to drive that point home. In the fog of the Red Triangle the perpetrator considers herself the expert, the only one who really sees the truth.

Often in a tirade or in a passive-aggressive swipe, she lets the other person know how stupid she thinks he is.

In our most primitive ego state, we spend all of our energy defending ourselves.

This primitive fight, flight, or freeze mechanism was helpful when it came to protecting ourselves from natural disasters and wild animals, but it is not very helpful when it comes to thriving in human relationships.

Our ego is dominantly preoccupied with survival. It works hard to establish comfort and certainty, and then it builds defenses to protect these values. If it is "right" about its certainty, then it can feel safe, in control, and in a position to judge the behaviors and actions of all living things. This is, of course, the age-old curse: man attempting to play the role of God.

When the ego is in control of our way of being, it produces a pervasive sense of fear and/or shame. While there are other emotions involved in the Red Triangle, these are the driving emotions for all three roles.

RESCUER   PERPETRATOR

fear
EGO
shame

VICTIM

The ego lives with the false belief that control and safety are fully achievable. In relationships, this is manifested in the ego's attempt to control the perception and behavior of others. If it can point out the inadequacies in someone else, it can avoid acknowledging its own insufficiencies.

What is the defining characteristic of the ego?

The ego or "pride" wants to avoid taking responsibility.

Does it want control? Yes.

Does it want to take responsibility? No.

Responsibility is vulnerable and intimate. Control is protective and shallow. Control is often masked as responsibility, but the difference is always revealed in the energy and outcome.

It is time for a party, and someone says, "I will take responsibility for decorations." Is that person really being responsible? Maybe. Perhaps she finds great joy in serving others and using her gift of hospitality as an expression of love to celebrate the other person.

Or perhaps she has a need to be in control. She has a very specific way in which they believe things should be decorated. If anyone attempts to adjust or thwart her vision of what she wants to create, she takes it personally. Her ego is offended. Her control has been challenged.

When finished, the ego, or "shadow self," wants people to notice the wonderful decorating job it did. It is hopeful that some of the attention that was meant to be directed to the person being celebrated would also be given to it.

Avoid
taking
responsibility

The ego longs to be recognized and validated by an outside source.

Why? Because the ego is fragile and is not empowered. It counts on others to establish its value.

In this way, the ego does not have to be responsible for itself.

If others do not act in accordance with the ego's expectations, then it can blame someone or something other than itself.

Brené Brown makes the point that "Blame is simply the discharging of discomfort and pain. It has an inverse relationship with accountability."[3]

We don't have to be angry with the ego or in despair of its activity in our lives. Its heightened sense of survival has kept us alive.

Unfortunately, that same preoccupation with surviving keeps us from thriving.

If the ego remains in control, one could make a huge impact on our world, yet the experience with intimacy could have been completely missed. There are stories of men and women who transformed the paradigms they lived in, yet took their own lives.

The ego blinds us from recognizing the beauty that surrounds us and the goodness that we leave behind.

Dwelling in the Red Triangle means that our relationships will not be characterized by a loving, robust, deep sense of connection, but instead will be a flat transactional experience that leaves us feeling empty and unseen.

(Scan this QR Code to listen in on an interview with one of my clients discussing being a perpetrator!)

THE RED TRIANGLE
IN ACTION

Here is an example of how the triangle works in common, everyday experiences:

Innocent question: "Did you wash the dishes?"

Response: "No."

Here are three ways the different types of people might respond to that answer:

Victim: "Of course you didn't. You never do anything I ask you to do. I have to do everything around this house."

Rescuer: "Well, it's not your fault. I should have reminded you. You have a lot on your mind. Don't worry about it. As soon as I take out the garbage, finish helping the kids with their homework, paint the stairwell, and invent a new form of fossil fuel, I will do it for you."

Perpetrator: "'No'? What do you mean 'No'?" Get your lazy butt off the couch and do what I asked you to do!

Which role do you find yourself in most often?

Which one is most tempting?

We have all danced in each of these corners of the Triangle at different times. We may have even moved through all three of them before breakfast!

You are not alone. We have each participated in this unhealthy way of relating! Humans are dynamic creatures. While everybody tends to have a preferred role in this Triangle, by nature we move around it. Tension builds in one or both people, and eventually it explodes, leaving our feelings scattered all over each other. Years of relating this way can leave us feeling as if a life full of drama will be a merry-go-round that will never end.

The way to stop the drama begins with one simple step:

Take ownership.

Take responsibility for your actions, reactions, behavior, and attitude.

INTENSITY VS. INTIMACY

The drama of the Red Triangle is all
about avoidance. We take up a posture
on the Red Triangle as a way of
manipulating the circumstances or the
other person to avoid being vulnerable
and taking ownership of our actions.

This avoidance behavior becomes highly addictive.

The primary reason for this is that addicts tend to confuse *intimacy* with *intensity*.

There is a rush that is experienced in the drama. The limbic system is in high gear. Our bodies respond to the intense emotions by releasing epinephrine. Our adrenaline is released, and we get amped.

Chemicals flow through our bodies, and the intensity of the drama is electrifying. We strategize and go to battle.

While this is intense and exhilarating, there is often a physical and emotional crash afterward.

Instead of creating solutions or a lasting connection, the drama only creates more confusion, and the violence left behind is a mosaic of battered emotions and fractured relationships—none of which are easily healed.

Life does not have to be this way. Choosing to take responsibility is the most powerful choice you will ever make.

If this is the case then why do we resist?
Why is it so hard to say, "I'm sorry."

At some point in our story we were
wounded by someone. At some point we
hurt someone else. As a child we don't
know how to fully process feelings like
hurt and shame. So we learn
mechanisms to avoid certain feelings.

A common avoidance strategy is push
pain down or push pain away.

PERSONALIZING
AND PROJECTING

One way to notice we are going Red is when we find ourselves continuously personalizing. We begin believing that everything that happens in our world is happening to us.

When a text isn't returned in a timely manner, we convince ourselves that the other person doesn't see us as important. When the cashier doesn't make eye contact with us, we think they are being rude.

When someone sets a boundary, we take it as a slight and believe we are not valued as we should be. We find ourselves taking everything personally.

Another reaction we can be wary of is projecting. When we feel insecure or inadequate, we are tempted to ascribe our fears and frustrations to others. Because we are fearful, we assume others should be fearful. We might even get angry because the other person is not as afraid as we are!

Personalizing and projecting are mechanisms we employ to avoid—you guessed it—taking responsibility.

That is understandable.

Responsibility is often a heavy burden. We do not want to bear the weight of being responsible for the way our attitudes and behaviors might impact others. This is the reason many of us play small. We hide, settle, and refuse the call of leadership.

The fears of hurting someone else and of being misunderstood have paralyzed many talented human beings.

While ducking responsibility might feel safe, it actually poses great danger to the soul. In our acquiescence to fear, we limit our experience with the expansiveness of love. Dancing in the drama, we are limited in our ability to access compassion.

Our physical receptors are tuned to protecting ourselves at all costs. Being vulnerable, open, and empathetic is literally the last thing on our minds. Toxic (recurring, relentless) drama keeps us far too self-absorbed in our own position of "rightness" to consider the feelings of the other person.

Actual problem-solving, which would promote growth and intimacy, fails to surface. Instead, the dance satiates the addictive nature of perceived control.

The manufactured intensity *temporarily* quenches the thirst for connection, but it is short-lived.

An eggshell stained in fear or shame is always nearby, and it won't be long before it is stepped on, triggering another furious round of suffering on the Red Triangle.

AWAKENING

When the suffering becomes unbearable, when we finally awaken to our inability to control our external world (often called "hitting our bottom"), or when we are offered incomprehensible grace in the face of our fury—then we are finally receptive to a new way of relating.

This psychological or spiritual experience is where we undergo an "awakening" to our true self and a death blow to the ego. Ultimately, we relinquish control.

Spiritual teachers call this a surrender to Presence.

To put it in the language of the Twelve Steps, we admit that we are powerless and that our lives have become unmanageable, and we choose to believe that a power greater than ourselves can restore us to sanity.

Fed up with managing the ego, we are presented with a pathway toward healing. This path is narrow. This path requires faith and trust. This path leads into the unknown, beyond our illusions of certainty and control.

This Thrivalist way of being is mystical
and full of wonder. The intimacy we
long for is only discovered in the wild.

It is only experienced in the wide-open,
untamed land of trust and vulnerability.
Vulnerability is where you find
compassionate power.

As Brené Brown said, "To love someone fiercely, to believe in something with your whole heart, to celebrate a fleeting moment in time, to fully engage in a life that doesn't come with guarantees— these are risks that involve vulnerability and often pain. . . . The discomfort of vulnerability teaches us how to live with joy, gratitude, and grace."[4]

Vulnerability's power is on display when we surrender, awaken to our true self, and take ownership of our experiences.

TRUE SELF

"True self" is a phrase used by psychologists, spiritual teachers, and quantum physicists to refer to the aspect of the Divine in each of us. This is your "higher self," "oneness with God," or "connection with Source." This is you as the "imago Dei" or "child of God."

Describing the spiritual journey, St. Teresa of Avila said, "This journey is a process of dismantling the monumental illusion that God is distant or absent."[5]

There is never a place to *get*; there is only a place to *be*.

God is not a being among beings, but rather is Beingness itself. When you begin to connect with God or Source as a verb rather than as a noun, all the limiting constructs we have placed around the Divine begin to fall away.

Stop trying to connect with God as a judge or grandfather type somewhere beyond the clouds, and start recognizing that the Divine is speaking in you, through you, and at times, as you.

As Marilyn Schlitz wrote, "We are born of the whole, and so even now, in our state of limited experience, we are still whole, still complete, but we are just not aware of that. When we become aware, we simply lose limitedness and become whole again."[6]

You are not stupid, bad, or worthless.

You have nothing to defend.

You were created in love, by love, and for love.

"The True Self . . . puts little trust in its private virtue, and feels no undue surprise at its personal weakness. . . . It is a reverence humming within you that must be honored."[7]

A pretty good working definition of love is "presence."

Be here now.

Open your eyes to the wonder of
possibility that surrounds you.

Heaven is already here. Love is a breath
away.

Eternity is not perpetual future, but perpetual presence.

Whatever the present moment contains, welcome it as your teacher. "Accept it as if you had chosen it. Always work with it, not against it."[8]

Access your divine gift, your
superpower:

Choice.

No one can take this from you.
Regardless of how hard your external
circumstances seem, you have the ability
to choose your mindset.

You can choose to love or not love, to
forgive or not forgive, to hate or not
hate, to smile or not smile.

You get to make meaning around your
experience.

Viktor Frankl, psychologist and Holocaust survivor, wrote, "We who lived in concentration camps can remember the men who walked through the huts comforting others, giving away their last piece of bread.

They may have been few in number, but they offer sufficient proof that everything can be taken from a man but one thing: the last of the human freedoms—to choose one's attitude in any given set of circumstances."[9]

HAVE TO OR GET TO?

With this reminder about the power of choice, you get to check in on your motivation.

Are you living from guilt, shame, reaction, codependency, obsession with validation, acknowledgement, or approval? Or are you living from vulnerability, curiosity, or gratitude?

Be honest enough with yourself to check in on your motivation.

Ask yourself, "Am I pleasing or am I serving?"

There is a big difference.

Dusan Djukich reminds us of this tragic truth: "Approval seeking is a toxic addiction. . . . The next morning, after all you've done to win someone over, you have no idea who they will decide to be with you."[10] What a waste of your precious energy!

Ask yourself, "Do I *have to* do this, or do I *get to* do this?"

Do you feel the difference in the energy?

"Have to" is stamped with compulsion and dread. "Get to" is flavored with interest and pleasure.

How you answer that question dramatically shapes your experience of the present moment.

I am accessing this mindset as I write: Do I have to finish this book, or do I get to finish this book?

"Have to" is loaded with pressure and procrastination. "Get to" is infused with hope and a deep desire that something that takes shape on these pages will bring relief, validation, meaning, confidence, and hope to my readers.

What about you?

Do you "have to" go to work, or do you "get to"?

Do you "have to" drive your kids, or do you "get to"?

Do you "have to" pick up groceries, or do you "get to"?

When you see your freedoms as a privilege, when you find pleasure in the mundane, and when you enjoy taking responsibility, you are exercising your greatest gift:

Choice.

Remember this about choosing: whatever it is you choose, and whatever happens after you choose—you get to choose again.

When you are attentive to your own wants and desires, when you embrace the sensuality of life rather than run from it, and when you say you're sorry for the impact you had on someone else, you are on your way to discovering deep, passionate, meaningful, and lasting relationships.

In your true self, there are three specific, healthy ways of relating that will produce this kind of flourishing.

These ways of relating are what make up the Green Triangle.

THE
GREEN TRIANGLE

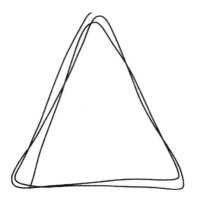

Have you ever heard someone say, "I am living my truth"? What is truth? Is it what we believe? If so, how do we explain why our beliefs shift and change over the years?

A belief is an abstract thought, an approximation of truth, a synapse firing in the brain.

What's true for us is not *what* we believe.
What's true for us is *how* we behave.

Several years ago I was a participant in
a program called, *Living Centered.* It was
hosted by a team of therapists at a place
near Nashville, Tennessee called,
"Onsite." The folks there introduced me
to the Green Triangle.

In the Green Triangle, the preoccupation shifts from proving what's right and what's wrong to a completely different energetic paradigm. Instead of playing a winner/loser game of right and wrong, consider the Thrivalist way:

Go Green.

OWNERSHIP

NEGOTIATION   BOUNDARIES

Start with these questions:

- What is true?

- What does this challenge/ conflict/experience bring up in me? What do I feel?

- What need or want is being identified? What is my request?

- Is this honoring to myself and others?

This way of being is characterized by curiosity and agency (power of choice). The right or wrong dilemma often takes you back to childhood, where at times you felt powerless and punishable.

Curiosity and choice remind you that you are an adult empowered, responsible, and capable of trusting your true self.

Kurt Hahn, founder of Outward Bound, wrote the following to young adventurers: "There is more in us than we know. If we could be made to see it, perhaps for the rest of our lives we will be unwilling to settle for less."[11]

Grounded in your true self, you begin to see the world not through scarcity, but through abundance.

Opportunity surrounds you.

A Thrivalist trades comfort for possibility, swaps judgment for curiosity, and exchanges control for vulnerability.

OWNERSHIP

OWNERSHIP

At the top of the Green Triangle is the empowered stance of Ownership. It is the opposite of Victim. Instead of pushing the blame on someone or something else, it's acknowledging your own inability to live out an ideal.

When triggered into the Red Triangle, you get to acknowledge the part you played in the drama.

Instead of saying, "I'm only late because my alarm didn't go off," or "It's not my fault I am late; traffic was crazy," or "My spouse misplaced my keys," you say, "I'm sorry I'm late."

Can you feel the difference in the energy? There is no need for excuses or reasoning when you take ownership.

A good way to remember this is a phrase I once heard from a friend:

"Adults announce; children explain."

Your time spent qualifying and contextualizing is often a result of your ego showing up in its immaturity, hoping that the explanation will cause the other person to be less disappointed with you.

A simple statement of ownership lets the other person know that you are an adult who does not expect perfection, but rather welcomes his own imperfection and failure as feedback for living.

Peter Crone has said, "Life will present people and circumstances to reveal where you're not free."[12]

When we take ownership, we see all of life as our teacher.

FAILURE

Failure is not something to avoid or feel ashamed of; failure is feedback. It is a gift.

It shows us which way *not* to go.

There is a famous story about Thomas Edison. It is said that he refined the invention of the light bulb "So many times it took him 10,000 attempts to perfect. However rather than accepting failure 9,999 times he is quoted as answering questions on his failures as rather: 'I have not failed. I have just found 9,999 ways that do not work.'"[13]

Failure is the evidence of our agency
and our willingness to take a risk and
step into a world of uncertainty. When
our failure has harmed someone else, we
feel sorrow rather than shame. We hurt
for them and with them, and then we
move on to the next moment.

We acknowledge that we made a
mistake, but that does not mean that we
are the mistake.

You are only the victim or perpetrator
of your own misstep the moment you
"miss" stepped.

The next moment, you are no longer the victim or perpetrator.

The action is not your identity.

It is a "miss-behavior" or a "miss-take." You missed the mark.

Acknowledge where and how you missed. Apologize for the impact it had on yourself or the other person.

Take responsibility for your action, and step forward with confidence into life again.

You and I are walking contradictions.

In the words of Captain Jack Sparrow, "You can accept that your father was a pirate and a good man, or you can't; but pirate is in your blood . . . , so you'll have to square with that someday."[14]

None of us is always good or always bad. We are saint and sinner simultaneously.

We are light and shadow. Try as we might during this earth walk, we will never snip the shadow away. It will always be there.

Carl Jung captures this eloquently:

"By bearing the opposites we can expose ourselves to life in our humanity. . . . We have to risk life to get into life, then it takes on color, otherwise we might as well read a book."[15]

Ours is not a journey into perfection; ours is a journey toward wholeness.

In a way, you might consider yourself a divine "Being" and a human "Becoming."

You have been created by God, so you are an expression of the Divine; yet you are created, so you are as an energetic becoming. Quantum physics has taught us that the observer is always influencing its reality. We are not a stagnant entity, but are rather a collection of experiences that finds its identity in relation to what surrounds us.

We like to name, categorize, and quantify, but none of this ever resolves what is true about our experience.

We are always changing; always becoming; always evolving.

The more you let go of your ego and live into your true self, the more you reconnect to the present, and the more you become whole.

"We are born with only one obligation—
to be completely who we are
[becoming].[16]

NEGOTIATION

NEGOTIATION

A friend of mine once said to me, "It's nice to be wanted; it's not nice to be needed."

Punchy, but so true! We have all been around people who come across as needy. We have been that person ourselves at different times. The harsh reality is that neediness is off-putting, unattractive, and sometimes even repelling.

Rather than asking for what you need, ask for what you want. It is more empowering.

Listen to your longings. Pay attention to your preferences. Instead of repressing desire or manipulating someone to get what you want, make a request. Ask.

Jesus once said, "Ask and it will be given to you; seek and you will find."[17]

Instead of perpetrating when you negotiate, stay true to the dignity of your humanity and the humanity of the other person.

This means that you will not intimidate, berate, or manipulate the other person to meet your desires, but rather, you will invite the other person to participate in the fulfillment of your desires.

They do not exist to meet your needs.

They can, however, if they choose to do so, contribute to your wants and participate in your preferences.

In one of her insightful TED Talks, Esther Perel speaks to this: "There is no neediness in desire. Nobody needs anybody."[18]

In communicating desire, we honor the dignity of the other person.

They can say "Yes," or they can say "No."

We have the privilege of sharing and negotiating what we value.

In choosing to name our preferences and feel our feelings, we acknowledge that connection with others is important to us.

In this way, we avoid getting on the Red Triangle and living only in relation to the needs and wants of others.

In a romantic relationship, overfunctioning for the other person creates a parent/child energy that does not serve the relationship well. Esther Perel goes on to say, "There is no caretaking in desire. Caretaking is overfunctioning. It's a powerful anti-aphrodisiac. I have yet to see somebody who is so turned on by somebody who needs them."[19]

This seems so simple, yet is so difficult. Why?

Because wanting is vulnerable. Wanting is an acknowledgment that you are not your own sustenance. You are interdependent on others for fulfillment.

Negotiation is about connection. It is about being true to your own longings while understanding and appreciating that the other person also has longings!

Simple and beautiful, this way of relating is completely lost when immersed in the drama of the Red Triangle.

It is impossible to be empathetic and compassionate when your ego believes it must fight, judge, defend, or run to preserve itself.

This way of going green is an invitation for the other person to be true to himself while you take responsibility for being true to yourself.

You are essentially saying to the other person,

"You may or may not be able to fulfill my wish, but I have enough inherent value to ask, and you have enough inherent value to respond."

EXPECTATIONS AND AGREEMENTS

You are letting go of expectations and replacing them with agreements.

Instead of trying to manage the other person, you now manage the agreement.

You both risk disappointing each other, and you both take a bold step toward trust.

"Without a question, an answer is experienced as manipulation. Without a struggle, help is considered interference. And without the desire to learn, the offer to teach is easily felt as oppression.

Therefore, our first task is not to offer information, advice, or even guidance, but to allow others to come into touch with their own struggles, pains, doubts, and insecurities—in short, to affirm their life as quest."[20]

When you choose to negotiate, you acknowledge that the other person's wants are as important as your own.

Occasionally, the pleasure of your wants will be perfectly in sync with the other person's wants.

At other times, your desires will oppose the other person's desires.

Acknowledge this—not as one person being right and the other person being wrong—but as two very different human "becomings" experiencing desire.

When you stop judging the other person for what they want and take responsibility for what you want, you will find yourself standing squarely in the green space of negotiation.

Here is an example:

Many of us grew up with the conventional wisdom that said, "Never go to bed angry."

While that is ideal, there will be times
when someone in the relationship is at
the bottom of their emotional tank.
Discussing, arguing, or fighting when
energy is low and when the primal,
lizard part of the brain has taken over is
not optimal for nuanced communication.

The discussion often descends into the ego, and one person, in frustration, pulls the emotional rip cord and abruptly exits the conversation.

A better solution might be to use negotiation.

For example, instead of saying, "Stop pressuring me. I can't have this discussion. I'm exhausted, and I'm going to bed," you could say, "I'm tired and do not have the energy to show up for either of us right now. I value your thoughts and feelings and would like to hear them. Would it work for us to finish this conversation in the morning over coffee?"

By making this simple adjustment, you have taken responsibility for your physical state and have made a request.

You have offered the other person an opportunity to take part in the decision.

If the other person joins you in the green space of negotiation, your responsibility is to keep your agreement the following morning.

However, if the other person moves to the Red Triangle and refuses to negotiate, your best option is to move to the third corner of the Green Triangle: Boundaries.

BOUNDARIES

BOUNDARIES

When you "go green," you learn how to engage in conflict in healthy ways.

You cannot limit or control the other person.

He or she has the freedom of choice, but what you can do is set limits on yourself.

Another word for this kind of constraint is the word "boundaries."

Healthy boundaries are like stone fences that outline your identity.

As Henry Cloud and John Townsend explain, "Boundaries are anything that helps to differentiate you from someone else, or shows where you begin and end. . . . Boundaries help us to define what is *not* on our property and what we are *not* responsible for."[21]

Setting boundaries is not saying, "You are not going to talk to me like that!" Rather, setting boundaries is saying, "If you continue to yell at me, I will remove myself from this conversation."

You cannot control someone else's boundaries, but you can determine your own.

You can decide your own plan of action.

You know your limits and the things that will trigger you into the Red Triangle.

You get to choose.

Rather than becoming a rescuer, you get to honor your own authority as a person of agency. Consider what is best for you, your partner, and the relationship—and make a decision.

Instead of trying to control the other person, you might expand on your boundaries and add negotiation by saying something like this: "If you are going to talk to me in that tone, then I will step away and will not continue to engage in this discussion for now. I still desire resolution. Would it work for you to continue this conversation tomorrow morning?"

It takes twenty minutes for the limbic system (that primal, lizard brain we mentioned) to cool down and reset. It is reasonable to let your partner or counterpart know that you want a break before things get too heated.

Be careful, however, that you don't use this as an excuse to avoid conflict and ignore your own needs, wants, and desires.

Avoidance is a sure sign that you have left ownership and have slid into the red corner of rescuer.

Be aware, though, that if you hit "pause," it is also your responsibility to hit "play." This is about working through conflict and getting through difficult moments in your relationships so that you can grow—both as an individual and as an interdependent partnership.

It is important to pay attention to your capacity.

Check your emotional fuel gauge.

Know what you are capable of in the moment. Make a decision.

A Thrivalist chooses to be the action rather than the reaction.

There may come a day when you are feeling fragile and you are anticipating walking into a difficult situation or having an encounter with someone who tends to cycle the Red Triangle.

Be clear about what you want.

You might begin the conversation by saying something such as, "I only have five minutes, but I wanted to reply to your request. Are you available?"

You are setting boundaries from the beginning, as opposed to shifting in the middle of a heated moment.

It is much harder to draw the boundary lines while you are caught in the red cycle.

Setting these types of boundaries keeps you from entering the drama cycle. Once you have set a boundary, you can negotiate an alternative time frame, or you can abide by it.

It's okay to live by the constraints you set.

If you try to live by everyone else's expectations, you will pay a steep emotional price.

As Dusan Djukich said, "Victims are fixated on solving the past. They nurture past hurts and memories. Owners focus on creating the future."[22]

Society will try to push you into a mold. It can take away all kinds of things from you.

Remember, that the one thing others can never take from you is your ability to choose how you see and where you place your focus.

You have the power to choose how you will see yourself, others, and the world around you.

Your perception is your responsibility.

It cannot be taken from you; it can only be relinquished.

Since the Red Triangle sets off the limbic system of your brain, putting you in fight, flight, or freeze mode, your goal is to get on the Green Triangle and get grounded in your ability to make choices.

Taking ownership, setting boundaries, and entering negotiation are mature, adult ways to get curious and ask for what you want while effectively managing your emotions.

Remember: adults announce and children explain. When you find yourself monologuing to defend your position, consider whether or not you are in your childish ego-self looking for validation from the other person.

This is often where you can lose yourself and abandon your empowered position of ownership.

Context and information can be helpful, but check in on your energy. Are you defensive?

Where there is self-love, there is no need for an explanation.

No one else gets to determine whether or not you are lovable.

You are already loved.

You came from Source. You are a child of God, an expression of the Divine.

You do not need the acceptance of others to define your existence.

You express your divinity by taking responsibility and making a choice.

THERE IS NO TRY

Choose and choose again. Remove the word "try" from your language. "Try" is simply a deflecting device that keeps you from taking full responsibility.

Choose and keep choosing.

If you are unsuccessful, remember that failure is simply feedback.

You learn, you adjust, you shift, you evolve, you become—and you keep choosing.

You are intentionally caring for your own soul.

You are actively stepping into the unknown. Let go of your fear of control and acknowledge your fear of loss.

"You can only lose something that you have, but you cannot lose something that you are."[23]

In *Atomic Habits*, James Clear reminds us that our focus gets to be on becoming the person of quality we want to be rather than the outcome we want to get.[24]

Decide on the person you want to be, and then practice being that person.

It is time for new habits—new neural pathways.

My psychologist friend Dave says, "As soon as you begin ruminating, ask yourself,

'Is this thought helpful?'"

For example, you might think, "The government is tracking and recording everything about my life." Well, if you are a senator, a lobbyist, a spy, or a government agent and you can do something about this, then this thought might be really helpful.

However, what if you are a homemaker and this thought preoccupies your mind for large portions of the day?

The thought may not necessarily be right or wrong, but is it helpful? Are there better uses of your time and energy?

Are you tired of toxic relationships?

Are you exhausted enough from doing the drama dance that you're ready to transform into something new?

Transformation happens when the ashes
of your life become the soil of rebirth.

Mark Nepo, observing the eating and digesting processes of the buffalo, writes about our similar experience:

"The ever-humbling cycle of growing strong roots comes from eating what grows from our own shit, from digesting and processing our own humanity."[25]

No one can take your joy; it can only be surrendered.

Get off the drama dance floor and stop being the rescuer.

Instead of losing yourself in the needs of the people around you, ask them to be clear about what they want. You might be surprised at how well this works.

It's time to take ownership of your wants and preferences.

What do you long for?

In what do you delight?

What fills you with awe and wonder?

What makes you come alive?

Cultivate these things, experiences, and relationships, as this is what the world is waiting for from you!

Please—come alive!

BE ACCOUNTABLE TO YOURSELF

This is your story. No one else gets to live your life. Only you do.

Are you ready to thrive?

Is there someone in your life you wish would leave the Red Triangle and join you in the green? If you choose to share these concepts or buy a friend a book, it is important to remember that the spirit of the Red Triangle is "demand," and the spirit of the Green Triangle is "invitation."

Do not tell someone what position they are in on the triangles, but instead ask them where they see themselves.

Whether you agree with their assessment or not, your question is in itself an invitation to the other person to take ownership.

Most importantly, choose to model what it looks like to live the life of a Thrivalist.

Ask yourself these questions:

- What am I responsible for?

- What am I not responsible for?

- What is the most powerful (responsible) choice I can make right now?

- My life is not a thing. It is an experience. What is emerging in me right now? What is begging to come out?

- Who am I becoming?

- When I feel stuck, it is only because there is an action I have been unwilling to take. What is that action?

While we are still together will you be
accountable to yourself? Will you use
your superpower? If so make an
agreement with yourself.

Today I make the choice. Today I will:

_____

_____

_____

_____

_____

_____

_____

_____

_____

Today I choose to become a Thrivalist!

(Name) _____

(Date) _____

Scan the QR code here to add your name to The Thrivalist Community!

Welcome to the Thrivalist community. Now, with your head up, your chest out, and standing strong on your own two feet, face the day, and enjoy the moments being strung out in front of you.

Go and thrive!

REFERENCES

[1] Anthony de Mello, *The Way to Love: The Last Meditations of Anthony De Mello* (New York: Crown Publishing Group, 1995), 21.

[2] Esther Perel, "The Secret to Desire in a Long-Term Relationship." TED, February 2013, https://www.ted.com/talks/esther_perel_the_secret_to_desire_in_a_long_term_relationship

[3] Brené Brown, "The Power of Vulnerability," RSA, Speech delivered on July 4, 2013, YouTube video, accessed April 11, 2022, https://www.youtube.com/watch?v=sXSjc-pbXk4.

[4] Brené Brown, *The Gifts of Imperfection* (Random House Inc, 2020), 97.

[5] Thomas Keating, *The Divine Indwelling: Centering Prayer and Its Development* (New York: Lantern Books, 2001).

[6] Marilyn Mandala Schlitz, *Living Deeply* (Oakland: New Harbinger Publications, 2008), 21.

[7] Richard Rohr, *Immortal Diamond* (San Francisco: Josey-Bass Publications, 2013), 54–56.

[8] Eckhart Tolle, *The Power of Now: A Guide to Spiritual Enlightenment* (Berkeley, CA: Publishers Group West, 2004), 29.

[9] Viktor E. Frankl, *Man's Search for Meaning: The Classic Tribute to Hope from the Holocaust* (London: Rider, 2021).

[10] Dusan Djukich, *Straight-Line Leadership* (Fairfield, CA: CRA, 2015), 65, 71.

[11] Kurt Hahn, "Our Mission." Outward Bound–India Himalaya. Accessed April 11, 2022. https:// www.outwardboundindia.com/our-mission.html.

[12] Teamsoul, "This Is Why We Suffer (and This Is How We End Our Own Internal Suffering)," Fearless Soul, December 2, 2020, https://iamfearlesssoul.com/ peter-crone-this-is-why-we-suffer-and-this-is-how-we-end-suffering/.

[13] Scott Cowley, "Thomas Edison and Michael Jordan Were Failures," *Insider*, September 16, 2010, https:// www.businessinsider.com/thomas-edison-and-michael-jordan-were-failures-2010-9.

[14] *Pirates of the Caribbean: The Curse of the Black Pearl*, directed by Gore Verbinski (Burnbank: Buena Vista Pictures, 2003), DVD.

[15] William McGuire, ed., *The Freud/Jung Letters* (Princeton: Princeton University Press, 1974), 94–95.

[16] Mark Nepo, *The Book of Awakening* (Newburyport, MA: Red Wheel, 2020), 11.

[17] Matthew 7:7, New International Version, BibleGateway.com.

[18] Esther Perel, "The Secret to Desire in a Long-Term Relationship." TED Talk.

[19] Perel, "Secret."

[20] Henri J. M. Nouwen, *Spiritual Direction: Wisdom for the Long Walk of Faith* (New York: HarperOne, 2015).

[21] Henry Cloud and John Sims Townsend, *Boundaries* (Grand Rapids: Zondervan, 2004).

[22] Dusan Djukich, *Straight-Line Leadership*, 116.

[23] Eckhart Tolle, *A New Earth: Awakening to Your Life's Purpose* (London: Penguin Books, 2018).

[24] James Clear, *Atomic Habits* (New York: Random House, 2018), 40.

[25] Mark Nepo, *The Book of Awakening*, 183.

Made in United States
Orlando, FL
06 November 2023

38645014R00107